A CALL TO DIE. A CALL TO LIVE.

FOLLOW ME

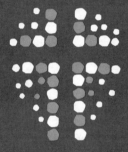

DAVID PLATT

LifeWay Press®
Nashville, Tennessee

Published by LifeWay Press®
© 2012 David Platt
Reprinted June 2013, September 2013, January 2014

ISBN 978-1-4158-7826-2
Item 005558770

Dewey decimal classification: 261.1
Subject headings: CHURCH \ CHRISTIAN LIFE \
CHRISTIANITY AND CULTURE

Photo of David Platt: Allison Lewis

To order additional copies of this resource, write to
LifeWay Church Resources Customer Service; One LifeWay
Plaza; Nashville, TN 37234-0113; fax (615) 251-5933;
phone toll free (800) 458-2772; order online at *www.lifeway.com*;
e-mail *orderentry@lifeway.com*; or visit the LifeWay
Christian Store serving you.

Printed in the United States of America

Student Ministry Publishing
LifeWay Church Resources
One LifeWay Plaza
Nashville, TN 37234-0144

CONTENTS

THE AUTHOR...4

1 THE CALL..5

2 BE TRANSFORMED.................................15

3 DELIGHT IN GOD...................................25

4 GOD'S WILL...35

5 THE CHURCH.......................................45

6 OUR MISSION.......................................55

PERSONAL DISCIPLE-MAKING PLAN......65

THE AUTHOR

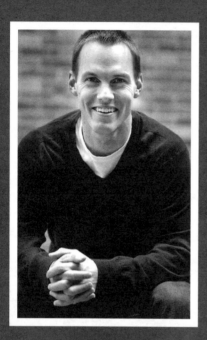

David Platt is the lead pastor of The Church at Brook Hills in Birmingham, Alabama. He is also the author of *Radical: Taking Back Your Faith from the American Dream* (Multnomah, 2010) and *Radical Together: Unleashing the People of God for the Purpose of God* (Multnomah, 2011). A well-known expositor, Platt holds three advanced degrees, including a doctorate from New Orleans Baptist Theological Seminary.

Platt's first love in ministry is spreading the gospel by making disciples. "I believe that God has uniquely created every one of his people to impact the world," he says. "God is in the business of blessing His people so that His ways and His salvation might be made known among all peoples." To this end Platt has traveled throughout the United States and around the world, teaching the Bible and training church leaders.

SESSION 1
THE CALL

THE CALL

Four fishermen stood by a sea in the first century when Jesus approached them. "Follow Me," He said, "and I will make you fishers of men." With these words, Jesus beckoned these men to leave behind their professions, possessions, dreams, ambitions, family, friends, safety, and security. He bid them to abandon everything. "If anyone is going to follow Me, he must deny himself," Jesus would say repeatedly.

In a world where everything revolves around self—protect yourself, promote yourself, preserve yourself, take care of yourself—Jesus said, "Slay yourself." And that's exactly what would happen. According to Scripture and tradition, these four fishermen paid a steep price for following Jesus. Peter was hung upside down on a cross, Andrew was crucified in Greece, James was beheaded, and John was exiled. Yet they believed it was worth the cost. In Jesus, these men discovered a love that surpassed comprehension, a satisfaction that superseded circumstances, and a purpose that transcended every other possible pursuit in this world. They eagerly, willingly, and gladly lost their lives in order to know, follow, and proclaim Him. In the footsteps of Jesus, these first disciples found a path worth giving their lives to tread.

Two thousand years later, how far from this path have we wandered? Somewhere along the way, amid varying cultural tides and popular church trends, it seems that we have minimized Jesus' summons to total abandonment. Churches are filled with supposed Christians who seem content to have a casual association with Christ and seem content to give nominal adherence to Christianity. Scores of men, women, and children have been told that becoming a follower of Jesus simply involves believing certain truths or saying certain words. But this is not true. Disciples like Peter, Andrew, James, and John show us that the call to follow Jesus is not simply an invitation to pray a prayer; it's a summons to lose your life. There is more to Jesus than the routine religion we are tempted to settle for at every turn, and experiencing biblical discipleship begins with answering the call.

Complete the viewer guide below as you watch DVD session 1.

When we come to Matthew 4:19, we see Jesus saying to four fishermen, "Follow Me."

Who is the "Me" that's going to be followed here?

Jesus is worthy of far more than church attendance and casual _____.

He is worthy of total abandonment and supreme _____.

What does the word "Follow" mean?

To live with radical _____ for His glory.

You become a follower of Jesus, and you lose _____ _____ as you know it.

We live for one thing: to honor the _____.

To follow Him is to live with urgent obedience to His mission.

Every follower of Jesus is a _____ of men.

Every disciple is a _____-_____.

> FROM THE VERY BEGINNING, FOLLOWING JESUS HAS ALWAYS INVOLVED FISHING FOR MEN. BEING A DISCIPLE HAS ALWAYS INVOLVED MAKING DISCIPLES.

When it comes to answering Jesus' call to follow Him, we discover that what He's really asking is for us to give up everything—literally, life as we know it—and die to ourselves. As we read about the first disciples of Jesus, it becomes abundantly clear that they were willing to walk away from everything that was familiar and natural to them.

> *As He was walking along the Sea of Galilee, He saw two brothers, Simon, who was called Peter, and his brother Andrew. They were casting a net into the sea, since they were fishermen. "Follow Me," He told them, "and I will make you fish for people!" Immediately they left their nets and followed Him.*
> *Going on from there, He saw two other brothers, James the son of Zebedee, and his brother John. They were in a boat with Zebedee their father, mending their nets, and He called them. Immediately they left the boat and their father and followed Him* (Matt. 4:18-22).

What was Jesus' specific statement to Peter, Andrew, James and John? How did they respond?

In the column on the left, make a list of the things the fishermen left behind according to Matthew 4:18-22. In the column on the right, list what each thing represented.

Left Behind
Boats

What It Represented
Profession/livelihood

What's changed in the 2000 years since Christ called those first disciples? Does Jesus still call us to leave everything behind and follow Him? Think about Christians today. Is it possible that we've begun to settle for routine religion rather than really living for Christ?

What excuses do Christians today often make that keep us from leaving everything behind as we answer Christ's call?

List people you know who have committed their lives to following Jesus. What have they left behind? Are you willing to do the same? Why or why not?

> TO FOLLOW JESUS MEANS TO LIVE WITH RADICAL
> ABANDONMENT FOR HIS GLORY.

When we really begin to look at what Jesus meant when He said, "Follow Me," we will discover far more pleasure to be experienced in Him, indescribably greater power to be realized with Him, and a much higher purpose to be accomplished for Him than anything else this world has to offer. And as a result, we will all—every single Christian—eagerly, willingly, and gladly lose our lives to know and proclaim Christ, for this is simply what it means to follow Him.

HOW DO YOU BECOME A CHRISTIAN?

Think about that question, "How do you become a Christian?" What comes to mind when you think about responding to Jesus' invitation to follow Him? How would you tell someone to begin following Jesus? Is it really as simple as walking an aisle and praying a prayer?

Read Matthew 4:18-22 again. Why do you think Jesus called Peter and Andrew to follow Him rather than just agree with certain truths about Him?

Sadly, today we have subtly and deceptively minimized what it means to follow Jesus. We have replaced challenging words like, "Leave everything and follow Me," with trite phrases like:
- *Ask Jesus into your heart.*
- *Invite Christ into your life.*
- *Pray this prayer after me, and you will be saved.*

Should it alarm us that the Bible nowhere mentions such a prayer? Should it concern us that nowhere in Scripture is anyone ever told to ask Jesus into their heart or invite Christ into their life?

How can these simple phrases lead to a misunderstanding of following Jesus?

Is it possible to profess Christ without knowing Christ? Explain.

"Not everyone who says to Me, 'Lord, Lord!' will enter the kingdom of heaven, but only the one who does the will of My Father in heaven. On that day many will say to Me, 'Lord, Lord, didn't we prophesy in Your name, drive out demons in Your name, and do many miracles in Your name?' Then I will announce to them, 'I never knew you! Depart from Me, you lawbreakers!' (Matt. 7:21-23)

According to this passage, who will enter the kingdom of heaven?

Why will Jesus say to some, "Depart from Me"?

These are truly difficult and challenging words from Jesus. There will be many who have believed they were followers of Jesus that will stand face-to-face with Him only to be told that they do not really know Him. Because of this, we should be very concerned about what the Bible does say about following Jesus.

RENOUNCE YOURSELF

In Matthew 4:17 Jesus begins His ministry on earth proclaiming, "Repent, because the kingdom of heaven has come near!" The word "repent" means to confess your sins and turn from them. Repentance is a rich biblical term that signifies an elemental transformation in someone's mind, heart, and life.

When people repent, they turn from walking in one direction to running in the opposite direction. From that point forward, they think differently, believe differently, feel differently, love differently, and live differently.

Have you chosen to follow Jesus? How did that journey begin for you?

In what ways have you begun to think differently, believe differently, feel differently, love differently, and live differently?

Write one response in each of the following categories below (follow the example):

	My life before repenting...	My life after repenting...
Thinking:	*How can I help myself?*	*How can I help others?*
Believing:		
Feeling:		
Loving:		
Living:		

HOW DO YOU KNOW THAT YOU ARE A CHRISTIAN?

"How do you know that you are a Christian?" Or, "How do you know that you are saved from your sin?" The most common replies to these questions from professing Christians are, "Because I decided to trust in Jesus," or "Because I prayed and asked Jesus to come into my heart many years ago," or even "Because I have given my life to Jesus." Such responses are not wrong, and I assure you my aim is not to be the word police, but I do want to offer what I hope is a healthy reminder that you and I are not saved from our sin primarily because *we* decided to do something however many years ago. Instead, we are saved from our sin ultimately because *Jesus* decided to do something two thousand years ago.

But surely the searching love of God must be believed and received. God is not the only one working in salvation, is He? A man or woman must choose to accept or reject the mercy of God in Christ, right? Absolutely. The mystery of God's mercy in no way negates the nature of man's responsibility. But the only way we can seek Christ in our sinfulness is because Christ first sought us.

Why is it important to recognize that Jesus initiates our salvation, and not us? What is our responsibility regarding salvation?

How do you know that you are a Christian, saved from your sin?

> WHEN WE ARE GLADLY WILLING TO LOSE
> OUR LIVES TO KNOW AND PROCLAIM CHRIST, WE HAVE
> ANSWERED THE CALL TO FOLLOW JESUS.

Read Luke 14:25-27.

Imagine a woman named Ayan. Ayan is part of a people who pride themselves on being 100% Muslim. Ayan's identity, familial honor, relational standing, and social status are all linked with Islam. Simply put, if Ayan ever leaves her faith, she will lose her life. If Ayan's family ever finds out that she is no longer a Muslim, they will slit her throat without question or hesitation.

Now imagine having a conversation with Ayan about Jesus. You start by telling her how God loves her so much that He sent His only Son to die on the cross for her sins as her Savior. As you speak, you can sense her heart softening toward what you are saying. At the same time, though, you can feel her spirit trembling as she contemplates what it would cost for her to follow Christ. With fear in her eyes and faith in her heart, she looks at you and asks, "How do I become a Christian?"

You have two options. One, you can tell her how easy it is to become a Christian. All you have to do is assent to certain truths, you might say. If Ayan will simply repeat a prayer, she can be saved.

Your second option is to tell Ayan the truth. You can tell Ayan that in the gospel, God is calling her to die. Literally.
- To die to her life.
- To die to her family.
- To die to her friends.
- To die to her future.

And in dying, to live. To live in Jesus. To live as part of a global family that includes every tribe. To live with friends who span every age. To live in a future where joy will last forever.

Ayan is not imaginary. She's a real woman I once met who made a real choice one day to become a Christian—to die to herself and to live in Christ, no matter what it cost. Because of her decision, she was forced to flee her family and friends. Yet she is now working strategically and sacrificially for the spread of the gospel among her people. The risk is high as every day she dies to herself all over again in order to live in Christ.

Put yourself in Ayan's shoes. How hard would it be to choose to follow Jesus?

Reflect on your own call to follow Jesus. What did you leave behind to follow Him?

How will your decision to follow Jesus impact your life and the lives of others today?

Pray that God will draw you closer to Him as you leave the things of the world behind and follow Jesus.

Read Galatians 4:4-5.

Cody is a member of our church who moved to Thailand to share the gospel with college students. One night, a student named Annan invited Cody to go to a movie. The two of them arrived and sat down in the theater to watch the film, but before it began, a video was shown about the king of Thailand. Immediately, everyone in the theater rose and applauded, including Annan. Some people began to cry tears of joy. As this short video played, people were visibly moved simply by the sight of their king on the screen.

When the movie ended and Cody and Annan walked out of the theater, Cody asked, "Why did everyone react with such emotion when the video about the Thai king was played?"

Annan responded, "Oh, Cody, we love, respect, and honor our king, for he is a king who cares for his people." He continued, "Our king will often leave his palace and come to villages and communities in Thailand to be with the people—to know them and identify with them. We know that our king loves the Thai people, and we love him."

As Cody listened, he knew that this description was setting the stage for him to share the story of a much greater King. In the days to come, Cody told Annan about how God, the King over all the universe, loved us so much that He came to us in the person of Jesus. He came to identify with us, even to the point of taking all of our sin upon Himself in order to save us and to make it possible for us to follow Him. Upon understanding this glorious reality, Annan became a follower of Jesus—not because he had been pursuing King Jesus, but because he realized that King Jesus had pursued him.

As you prepare for next week's session, reflect on the truth that Jesus came to us. He came to earth as a man to extend God's grace and mercy to us. It is Christ in us that transforms our life and allows us to follow Him. As we follow Him, our lives will be transformed in every way, made into the likeness of His image.

What does it mean to be transformed? Have you ever seen someone's life become radically different after responding to Jesus' call to follow Him? When?

Consider your own life. What is one area that most needs to be transformed?

Pray, focusing on how following Christ and becoming more like Him can begin to transform your life today.

MIND GAMES

Following Christ comes with a cost that accompanies stepping out of casual, comfortable, cultural Christianity. Consider the thoughts and things of this world that we must let go of in order to follow Jesus. Perhaps you've heard the old saying "garbage in, garbage out" in reference to the things you watch, listen to, and participate in. In essence, this is referring to the things we give our time and attention to and how they affect our lives. If we look at pornography, it will shape the way we view sexuality. If we listen to music that glorifies an ungodly lifestyle, it will shape our view of how to live. Whether or not you agree with this saying, the Bible is clear in Philippians 4:8-9:

> *Finally brothers, whatever is true, whatever is honorable, whatever is just, whatever is pure, whatever is lovely, whatever is commendable—if there is any moral excellence and if there is any praise—dwell on these things. Do what you have learned and received and heard and seen in me, and the God of peace will be with you.*

Dwelling on these things will result in God's peace being with you. This week, try this experiment:

Filter everything you listen to and watch on TV, the Internet, or the movies through this Scripture passage. Intentionally plan to listen to music and watch TV shows that are honoring to God and reflect His truth and beauty. This may take some planning, so think it through.

Plan to read through and reflect on the following passages this week:

- Monday—*Isaiah 40:29*
- Tuesday—*Psalm 119:138*
- Wednesday—*Romans 8:35-39*
- Thursday—*1 John 2:5*
- Friday—*Hebrews 12:10*
- Saturday—*Psalm 107:9*
- Sunday—*Romans 8:31*

At the end of the week, answer these questions:

How has this week been any different than a "normal" week as a result of what I heard or listened to or what I saw?

What are some things I need to do differently to adjust how I fill my mind from this week forward?

How will I fill my mind with truth on a regular basis?

SESSION 2
BE
TRANSFORMED

BE TRANSFORMED

Imagine you and I set up a meeting for lunch at a restaurant, and you arrive before I do. You wait and wait and wait, but thirty minutes later, I still haven't arrived. When I finally show up, completely out of breath, I say to you, "I am so sorry that I am late. When I was driving over here, my car had a flat tire, and I pulled over on the side of the interstate to fix it. While I was fixing it, I accidentally stepped out into the road, and a Mack™ truck going about 70 miles per hour suddenly hit me head on. It hurt. But I picked myself up, finished putting the spare tire on the car, and drove over here."

If I told you this, you would know that I am either deliberately lying or completely deceived. Why? Because if someone is standing in the middle of a road and gets hit by a Mack truck, that person is going to look very different than he did before!

Similarly, once a person truly comes face-to-face with Jesus, the God of the universe in the flesh, and He reaches down into the depth of their heart, saves their soul from the clutches of sin, and transforms their life to follow Him, that person's life is going to look different. Very different.

Following Jesus leads to transformation. Once we have answered the call to follow Him, in order to truly be His disciple we need to first understand how that will change our life.

Complete the viewer guide below as you watch DVD session 2.

What three truths are found in the imagery of Christ as a vine and Christians as branches?

1. As a disciple of Christ, you are united with Christ.

As His disciple, you remain in Him and He remains in you, just like He remains in the _____ and the Father remains in _____.

As a disciple of Jesus, _____ is in you.

2. When you confess Jesus as Lord, He changes everything in your life.

A branch connected to the vine has _____ and bears _____.

Jesus transforms you from the _____ out.

Jesus turns you _____ down.

3. As we abide in His Word, we bear fruit in this world.

We remain in Jesus by letting His _____ remain in us.

"If you obey my _____, you will remain in my love, just as I have obeyed my Father's commands and remain in his love" (John 15:10, NIV).

Do I really believe the Word of God?

Being a disciple of Jesus automatically leads to _____ disciples of Jesus.

Believing the words of Jesus automatically leads to _____ the words of Jesus.

> IF YOU REALLY BELIEVE THE WORDS OF JESUS,
> AND YOU REALLY LIVE UNDER THE LORDSHIP
> OF JESUS, UNITED WITH CHRIST, OBEYING HIS WORD,
> THEN HE WILL LEAD YOU TO LIVE VERY DIFFERENTLY
> FROM THE REST OF THIS WORLD.

Jesus tells us in John 15 that as His disciple you remain in Him and He remains in you, just like Jesus remains in the Father and the Father remains in Him. Think about the weight of this for a moment. If you are a Christian, then Christ is in you and you are in Christ. He is with you, every moment of every day forever—and you are with Him… in His life, in His death, in His resurrection, and in His reign. This is astounding!

> *"I am the true vine, and My Father is the vineyard keeper. Every branch in Me that does not produce fruit He removes, and He prunes every branch that produces fruit so that it will produce more fruit. You are already clean because of the word I have spoken to you. Remain in Me, and I in you. Just as a branch is unable to produce fruit by itself unless it remains on the vine, so neither can you unless you remain in Me.*
> *"I am the vine; you are the branches. The one who remains in Me and I in him produces much fruit, because you can do nothing without Me. If anyone does not remain in Me, he is thrown aside like a branch and he withers. They gather them, throw them into the fire, and they are burned. If you remain in Me and My words remain in you, ask whatever you want and it will be done for you. My Father is glorified by this: that you produce much fruit and prove to be My disciples* (John 15:1-8).

According to this passage, how does a follower of Christ glorify God? Can we produce little or no fruit and still be His disciples? Explain.

How do you know if you are living a fruitful life as a follower of Christ?

When Jesus says, "Remain in Me, and I in you" He is summing up the essence of the Christian life. As a disciple of Christ, you are united with Christ.

Read the following verses and list the ways Christians are in Christ:

- 2 Timothy 3:12—We live *in* Christ.

- Ephesians 6:10—

- Philippians 1:14—

- Galatians 2:4—

- Philippians 4:7—

- Ephesians 1:12—

- 2 Corinthians 2:14—

Each Scripture makes it clear that Christians are in Christ. We also see in John 15 that as Jesus remains in us and we in Him, we will be transformed.

List the first three things that come to mind when you think of the word transformed:

1.

2.

3.

Transformation is something that happens in the life of every Christian as we remain in Jesus. To be transformed is to be changed from one thing into another. To change one way of thinking into another way. To change one way of feeling into another way.

AS WE ARE UNITED WITH CHRIST AS LORD, HE CHANGES EVERYTHING ABOUT OUR LIVES.

THE TRANSFORMATION

When you confess Jesus as Lord, He changes everything in your life. Everything. He forgives you of your sin and He fills you with His Spirit—literally, Christ in you. Just like the vine and the branch story from John 15, a branch that's on the ground looks very different from a branch that's connected to the vine. Jesus transforms your life from the inside out.

JESUS TRANSFORMS YOU FROM THE INSIDE OUT

Starting with the inner circle below, note the transformation Jesus makes in each area of our lives:

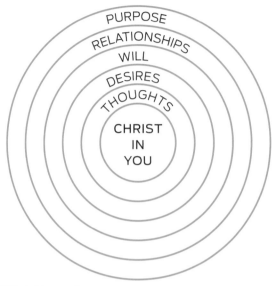

First (Inside) circle: "Christ in you"

As Christ dwells in us, He begins to transform everything about us.

Second circle: Thoughts

When we come to Christ He doesn't just give us a new heart, He gives us a new mind.
- *1 Corinthians 2:16*—We have the mind of Christ.
- *Romans 12:1-2*—We are transformed by the renewing of our minds.
- *2 Corinthians 10:5*—We take captive every thought to make it obedient to Christ.

How does a Christian think differently than the rest of the world?

Third circle: Desires

Christ dwelling in us transforms our desires, our feelings, and our affections.
The more we know Christ with our minds, the more we long for Christ in our affections.

How are a Christian's desires different from those of the world?

In what ways have your desires changed since becoming a follower of Jesus?

Fourth circle: Will

As we think like Jesus, and we desire what Jesus desires, then we act as Jesus would act. We live according to Jesus' will, not our own.

Do you agree or disagree with the following statements? Explain.

- The way we act is based on what we believe in our minds and what we desire with our emotions.

- We continue to fall into temptation because we fundamentally don't believe what God says.

Fifth circle: Relationships

When Christ dwells in us He transforms our thoughts, desires, will and the way we relate to the people around us. As a result of Christ remaining in us and us remaining in Him, our love for those around us grows.

> *This is My command: Love one another as I have loved you. No one has greater love than this, that someone would lay down his life for his friends* (John 15:12-13).

Who are three people you love and want to continue to grow in love toward as Christ works in you?

1.

2.

3.

Who is someone you find difficult to love? How can you grow in your love for them?

Sixth circle: Purpose

When our lives are transformed from the inside out, our thoughts, desires, will and relationships become totally different than the rest of the world, and our entire reason for living is turned upside down. Ultimately, this affects our purpose in the world. Remember, as a vine that remains in Jesus, we will bear fruit. That is His purpose for us as His disciples.

What is your purpose as a Christian? How will you live out your purpose this week?

THE CALL FROM CHRIST IS CLEAR: BELIEVE MY WORD, OBEY MY WORD, AND PROCLAIM MY WORD.

Read 1 John 1:9.

I heard a story once about an Englishman who bought a Rolls-Royce. It had been advertised as the car that would never, ever, ever break down. So, the man bought the Rolls-Royce at a hefty price and was driving it one day when, to his surprise, it broke down. He was far away from town so he called Rolls-Royce and said, "Hey, you know this car that will never break down? Well, it's broken down."

Immediately, a Rolls-Royce mechanic was sent via helicopter to the location where the car was broken down. The car was fixed, and the man went on his way. Naturally, the man expected to get a bill from Rolls-Royce. It was clearly expensive for them to provide such service (not often does a mechanic fly to where your car is broken down!) and he wanted to get the whole ordeal behind him. So when the bill had not yet come a few weeks later, the man called Rolls-Royce and said, "I'd like to go ahead and pay the bill for my auto repairs so that we can get this behind us." In turn, Rolls-Royce responded by saying, "Sir, we are deeply sorry, but we have absolutely no record of anything ever having gone wrong with your car."

Consider the wonder. For all who come to Christ and receive a new heart from Him, the God of the universe looks at you and says, "I have absolutely no record of anything ever having gone wrong in your life."

Have you fully embraced the fact that, in Christ, you are sinless in the eyes of God?

What is your response to God's grace in forgiving your sin?

How do you show mercy and grace to others in light of what God has done in your life?

Pray, thanking God for not keeping a record of your sins and giving you a new heart to live for Him.

Read Matthew 11:28-29.

God's law in the Old Testament commanded God's people not to travel on the Sabbath. Invariably, teachers of the law began to ask, "Well, what constitutes traveling? Can you travel around your house? Can you travel to someone else's house? If you travel beyond someone else's house, how far can you go?" In response, these teachers laid down a new law saying, "You can travel 3,000 feet from your house on the Sabbath. One exception to this is if you have food that is within 3,000 feet of your house to eat on the Sabbath. If that's the case, then that food is an extension of your house, and you can travel 3,000 feet from the place where your food is." Basically, if you put food in the right places, you could spend the Sabbath traveling all over town.

Similarly, the law said that you could not carry a load on the Sabbath. But the teachers asked, "What is considered a load? Are your clothes a load?" In turn, these teachers said that as long as you are wearing your clothes, they are not a load. But if you are carrying an item of clothing, it is considered a load. So it would be okay to wear a jacket on the Sabbath, but it would be wrong to carry a jacket on the Sabbath. In addition to such Sabbath regulations, all sorts of other rules dominated the day in which the disciples lived.

This background makes the words of Jesus in Matthew 11:28-29 all the more refreshing. They tenderly resound in a world where every other religious teacher says, "Try harder, work harder, do more, become better." Clearly our greatest need is not more regulations in order to merit salvation. Our greatest need is not to try harder. Our greatest need is a new heart.

Have you ever felt like you needed to try harder to be a Christian? Explain.

What is your first response when you read Matthew 11:28-29? What do you need rest from?

Why is it so important to give your burdens to Christ? How will you begin to do that?

Pray, asking God to help you remember that He will take your burdens and give you rest as you abide in Him.

FUEL

We may not have noticed it before, but there is a constant battle for our affection. We can choose to love the things of the world or we can set our hearts and minds on the things of God. Look closely at Colossians 3:1-4:

> *So if you have been raised with the Messiah, seek what is above, where the Messiah is, seated at the right hand of God. Set your minds on what is above, not on what is on the earth. For you have died, and your life is hidden with the Messiah in God. When the Messiah, who is you life, is revealed, then you also will be revealed with Him in glory.*

So, how do we fuel our affection for God when we tend to enjoy so many things in the world?

Think about someone you have a strong relationship with. List everything you can think of that makes this relationship so good.
For example: I look forward to talking to this person on the phone.

Think about how each of these aspects of your relationship fuels your affection for that person. For instance, you like to talk on the phone; conversation is one aspect that fuels your affection for them. List the various ways below:
For example: Conversation

Now apply each of these aspects to your relationship with God. These same things can help fuel your affection for Jesus as you follow Him.

In the week ahead, reflect on the importance of fueling your affection for Jesus in each of these different ways.

SESSION 3
DELIGHT IN GOD

DELIGHT IN GOD

When Jesus came on the scene in human history and began calling followers to Himself, He did not say, "Follow certain rules. Observe specific regulations. Perform ritual duties. Pursue a particular path." Instead, He said, "Follow Me." With these two simple words, Jesus made clear that His primary purpose was not to instruct His disciples in a prescribed religion; His primary purpose was to invite His disciples into a personal relationship. He was not saying, "Go this way to find truth and life." Instead, He was saying, "I am the way, the truth, and the life." The call of Jesus was, "Come to Me. Find rest for your souls in Me. Find joy in your heart from Me. Find meaning in your life through Me."

This extremely shocking and utterly revolutionary call is the essence of what it means to be a disciple of Jesus: we are not called to simply believe certain points or observe certain practices, but ultimately to cling to the person of Christ as life itself.

But we have missed this. In so many ways and in so many settings, we have relegated Christianity to just another choice in the cafeteria line of world religions. Slowly and subtly, we have let Christianity devolve into just another set of rules, regulations, practices, and principles to observe. Hindus bathe in the Ganges River; Christians get baptized in the church. Muslims go to worship on Friday; Christians go to worship on Sunday. Buddhists recite mantras; Christians sing choruses. Sikhs read their holy book and share with the needy; Christians read their Bibles and give to the poor. Now don't get me wrong: I am definitely not saying that we should not be baptized, sing in worship, read our Bibles, or serve the poor. But what I am saying is that if we are not careful, any one of us could do all of these things completely apart from Jesus.

Complete the viewer guide below as you watch DVD session 3.

We cannot separate faith in Christ from feelings for Christ.

God intends what we _____ _____ Him to create _____ _____ Him.

Christ alone can fulfill our desires.

Our deepest craving is not ultimately for something, but for _____.

Our satisfaction is not found ultimately in gifts, but in the _____.

Christ alone can transform our tastes.

We can conquer sin by trusting Christ to change our _____.

How will you and I overcome the pleasures of sin in this world? By letting Christ overcome us with the _____ of His satisfaction.

The Bottom Line:

We can live for the fleeting pleasures of this world, or we can live for _____ pleasure in our God.

> WHAT IF GOD INTENDS FOR YOU NOT ONLY TO *KNOW* HIM—
> WHAT IF GOD INTENDS FOR YOU TO *ENJOY* HIM?

A life of following Jesus leads to a desire for Him above all things.

We crave all kinds of things in life, and we were created by God to do so. From the very beginning God created man with needs, with wants, and with cravings. In Genesis 3 we see man and woman tempted by food on a tree that God had strictly forbidden them not to eat. Look at this picture of sin:

> *Then the woman saw that the tree was good for food and delightful to look at, and that it was desirable for obtaining wisdom. So she took some of its fruit and ate it; she also gave some to her husband, who was with her, and he ate it (Gen. 3:6).*

Eve saw that this fruit was *good* for food... and *pleasing...* and *desirable.* And for the first time, we see the cravings of man driving him to fulfill himself apart from God.

Think about all of the things you crave. What is it that makes you want them?

From the following list, what three things do you desire most?

❏ Chocolate   ❏ Ice cream   ❏ Video games
❏ Friends   ❏ Good conversation   ❏ Facebook time
❏ Sports   ❏ Dessert   ❏ A good book
❏ Cell phone   ❏ Instagram followers   ❏ A date for Friday night
❏ Approval   ❏ Sleep   ❏ Relationship with my parents
❏ Good grades   ❏ Music downloads   ❏ Other: _____

Although God has given us all kinds of good things we crave, such as food, recreation, and community, ultimately our cravings are designed to be satisfied by our Creator. The cravings we have should lead us to Jesus, not replace Him as the focus of our worship.

> *The next day, the crowd that had stayed on the other side of the sea knew there had been only one boat. They also knew that Jesus had not boarded the boat with His disciples, but that His disciples had gone off alone. Some boats from Tiberias came near the place where they ate the bread after the Lord gave thanks. When the crowd saw that neither Jesus nor His disciples were there, they got into the boats and went to Capernaum looking for Jesus.*
>
> *When they found Him on the other side of the sea, they said to Him, "Rabbi, when did You get here?"*
>
> *Jesus answered, "I assure you: You are looking for Me, not because you saw the signs, but because you ate the loaves and were filled. Don't work*

for the food that perishes but for the food that lasts for eternal life, which the Son of Man will give you, because God the Father has set His seal of approval on Him" (John 6:22-27).

Why did this crowd go looking for Jesus? What were they craving?

What food did Jesus promise them? Why?

With all of the good things Jesus has given us to enjoy, we can get caught up in trying to find our satisfaction in them. But our satisfaction is not ultimately to be found in the things we crave or desire; our satisfaction is ultimately intended to be found in Him.

> OUR SATISFACTION IS NOT FOUND IN GIFTS, BUT IN THE GIVER OF GIFTS: JESUS.

SUPERFICIAL RELIGION

Do you ever feel like Christianity consists of nothing more than a list of truths to believe and things to do? Do you ever find yourself weary in the process of trying to do it all? If we're not careful, we'll be consumed by trying to keep up with everything: quiet time, prayer time, Bible study, small groups, serving opportunities. Our faith becomes more of a duty than something we delight in.

This is the curse of superficial religion: the constant attempt to do outward things apart from inward transformation.

But what if God intends for you not only to *know* Him; what if God intends for you to *enjoy* Him?

What are some things we attempt to do in order to feel we are experiencing the Christian life?

1. *Example: I help serve food at a soup kitchen for the homeless.*

2.

3.

4.

5.

Now we must be careful here. Jesus has told us to do good things. He has called us to die to ourselves and live for Him. While the things we do in response to His commands are important and good, when those things become the focus of our faith rather than Jesus then we fall into error.

How can the good things you listed distract you from Jesus? How can you be sure they are the result of following Jesus and finding joy in Him?

How they can become my focus:
- *Serving in soup kitchen makes me feel better because I am helping the homeless.*

How they can lead to greater joy in Jesus:
- *I serve in the soup kitchen because it gives me the opportunity to share God's love with those in need.*

SUPERNATURAL REGENERATION

Jesus did not come so that we might live a life of superficial religion. He came so that we might receive new life through supernatural regeneration. Our greatest need is not to try harder. Our greatest need is a new heart.

Think back to the crowd following Jesus in John 6. They wanted their physical hunger satisfied. Rather than continuing to feed them, Jesus told them that if they wanted true and lasting satisfaction, not for their stomachs but for their souls, they needed to come to Him. Superficial religion will always leave us unfulfilled. Supernatural regeneration will always satisfy our deepest cravings as we find our joy in Christ.

> *Jesus said to them, "I assure you: Moses didn't give you the bread from heaven, but My Father gives you the real bread from heaven. For the bread of God is the One who comes down from heaven and gives life to the world."*
> *Then they said, "Sir, give us this bread always!"*
> *"I am the bread of life," Jesus told them. "No one who comes to Me will ever be hungry, and no one who believes in Me will ever be thirsty again* (John 6:32-35).

What are some things that you love or long for that are keeping you from a deeper love and greater longing for God?

What might you do, in faith, to cultivate a deeper desire for Jesus?

Are you engulfed in superficial religion or have you experienced supernatural regeneration? Explain.

Are you concentrating on Christian principles and practices in your life? If so, how can you move toward clinging to Christ as your very life?

There is no question that if you really believe the words of Jesus, and you really live under the lordship of Christ, obeying His Word, then He will lead you to live very differently from the rest of the world. Are you confident that you've been forgiven of your sin and is it clear that you are filled with His Spirit? Ultimately, have you been born again? The bottom line is this: we can live for the fleeting pleasures of this world or we can live for everlasting pleasure in our God.

> WE VIEW JESUS AS THE ONLY ONE WHO CAN SAVE
> US FROM OUR SINS, BUT WE FORGET THAT HE IS ALSO
> THE ONLY ONE WHO CAN SATISFY OUR SOULS.

on what you studied.

Read Matthew 28:16-20.

When I look at the church today, it seems like we have taken the costly command of Christ to go, baptize, and teach all nations and mutated it into a comfortable call for Christians to come, be baptized, and sit in one location. If you ask individual Christians today what it practically means to make disciples, you will likely get jumbled thoughts, ambiguous answers, and probably even some blank stares. We seem to have exempted one another from any personal responsibility to fish for men, and I'm convinced that the majority of professing Christians would not say their purpose in this life is to make disciples of all nations. In fact, most would shrink back from this thought, and some may even be tempted to give up on the very idea. This is no longer for me, you might think.

But please don't give up. Think about it with me. Biblically, isn't every single disciple of Jesus intended to make disciples of Jesus? From the very beginning of Christianity, hasn't following Jesus always involved fishing for men? And doesn't it seem like these early disciples of Jesus made disciples of Jesus not because they had to, but because they wanted to? Those first disciples on the mountain in Matthew 28 did not have to be superficially cajoled into making disciples; they were supernaturally compelled to do it. Not even death could stop them from obeying this command.

What is keeping us from obeying this command today? I mean every single one of us. Why are so many supposed Christians sitting on the sidelines of the church, maybe even involved in the machinery of the church, but not wholeheartedly, passionately, sacrificially, and joyfully giving their lives to following Christ and making disciples? Could it be because so many people in the church have settled for superficial religion instead of supernatural regeneration?

Do you think every single disciple is supposed to be making disciples? Why or why not?

What are you doing to make disciples?

Pray, asking God to transform everything about your life—and to stir in you a new desire to share the gospel and see people changed by His power.

Read Psalm 46:10.

A few years ago, my wife Heather and I traveled to a part of East Asia where very few people have ever heard of Jesus before. While we were there, Heather repeatedly shared the gospel with one particular girl named Meilin. On one hand, Meilin seemed so receptive to the gospel, yet clearly, something in her spirit was still resisting Christ as Lord. Amidst her many questions, we persistently prayed and pleaded for God to give us the words, wisdom, and grace needed to share the gospel clearly with Meilin.

After we had spent a couple of weeks with Meilin, it was time for us to leave her town. We packed our bags and said goodbye to the group of people who would be sharing the gospel there after we left. They were praying and studying the Bible just inside the home where we had been staying, and we could hear them talking while we waited outside for our ride.

At that moment, seemingly out of nowhere, Meilin rushed up to Heather. She pulled Heather aside and eagerly began to share how she was turning from her sin and trusting in Christ. Right as Meilin shared this and Heather celebrated with her, the group inside the house behind us— who had no idea what was going on outside the house—was reading Psalm 46:10 aloud. As I looked over and saw tears streaming down Heather's face as she prayed with Meilin, I heard the group inside the house saying these words: "Be still, and know that I am God. I will be exalted among the nations, I will be exalted in the earth" (NIV). Immediately, I was reminded that the Savior who reigns at the right hand of the Father is ready to give His disciples everything they need to exalt His name all over the world.

When has God provided you the opportunity to share the gospel?

Jesus wants to use you to advance His kingdom. Are you willing to write a "blank check" to God, giving Him your entire life as a disciple committed to following Him no matter what? If not, what is keeping you from fully following Him?

Pray that God will help you live every day prepared to give your life as a "blank check" for Him—to use you for His glory and the spread of the gospel.

SHARE THE LOVE

Go, therefore, and make disciples of all nations, baptizing them in the name of the Father and of the Son and of the Holy Spirit, teaching them to observe everything I have commanded you. And remember, I am with you always, to the end of the age" (Matt 28:19-20).

Jesus is clear in the Great Commission that every follower of His is to go and make disciples. This can be pretty intimidating, especially for an introvert. The good news is that there is nothing that limits us from sharing the gospel with those around us. It may simply mean that we need to be creative in how we share.

Let's take a look at how we can engage others and step into a Great Commission lifestyle.

Make a short list of your favorite things to do. (read, play football, watch TV, etc.)

Now list the things you are most knowledgeable about. (science, math, hunting, etc.)

Consider for a moment how the items you listed connect you with other people. For instance, if you play sports, think about the relationships you have with the other players. If you like to read, think about your friends who enjoy reading the same books you do. If you're a math whiz, think of all the people who might benefit from your help with the subject. Once you've made that connection, think of how you can sow seeds of the gospel in those relationships. Now commit to acting on all the different ways you can spread the love and grace of God with others as you simply go about your life.

SESSION 4
GOD'S WILL

GOD'S WILL

What is God's will for my life? This is quite possibly one of the most commonly asked questions in Christianity today. We have questions and we face decisions all the time, and we often find ourselves wondering about God's will in many of them.

Some decisions are small and seem less significant. What book should I read this month? Where should I eat today? What do I eat? Mexican? Chinese? Burgers? Italian? What do I do when my friend is mad at me? What do I do when my parents seem unhappy with me? What do I do when I am struggling?

Other questions involve large, life-altering decisions. Should I date? If so, who should I date? Should I go to college? If so, where? What should I major in? What career path should I choose? Should I marry? If so, who should I marry? Should we have kids? If so, how many kids? Where should I live? How should I live?

We find ourselves buried under a myriad of questions and decisions, and in the middle of it all we keep coming back to that one: What is God's will for my life? What does God want me to do? How do I find God's will for my life? We operate as if God's will is lost and we've devised an assortment of methods for finding it.

With good intentions, we try hard to use various methods to find the will of God. Like flipping through the Bible at random and putting a finger on a verse or looking for a sign like a burning bush or a blinding light. Maybe you look to coincidence and tie that to what God wants in your life.

But what if God's will was never intended to be found? In fact, what if it was never hidden from us in the first place? What if God the Father has not sent His children out on a cosmic Easter egg hunt to discover His will while He sits back in heaven saying, "You're getting colder… warmer… colder…"? And what if searching for God's will like this actually misses the entire point of what it means to be a disciple of Jesus?

Complete the viewer guide below as you watch DVD session 4.

One of the most common questions we ask as Christians in the contemporary church is, "What's God's will for my life?"

More important than knowing God's will for our lives is an unhesitating, unconditional commitment to _____ God's will for our lives. It's like giving God a blank check.

Ten reasons why we must give God a blank check with our lives and in our churches:

1. Jesus is worthy of absolute _____.

2. Jesus is working to advance His _____.

3. Jesus has clothed every single one of us with His _____.

4. Jesus has given every single one of us the same _____.

5. The world is our _____.

6. The Word is our _____.

7. The stakes are _____.

8. The Spirit is _____.

9. The glory of Christ leaves us no other _____.

10. The coming of Christ leaves us with great _____.

> HERE IS A BLANK CHECK WITH MY LIFE, GOD.
> WHATEVER YOU SAY, I WILL DO.

When Jesus says, "Follow Me," He's inviting us to totally surrender our lives, leave whatever He calls us to leave, and follow Him wherever He leads. Asking, "What's God's will for my life?" focuses on self: Where do I fit? What is my role? How does God fit into my plans? We need to make a fundamental shift to the real question, "Will I obey God's will for my life?"

Understanding the difference between these two questions leads us to give God a "blank check." Rather than spending our lives looking for God's will, which has already been given to us in the form of His Word, God invites us to say to Him, "Use me, lead me, guide me, do whatever you want in and through me to make Your gospel and Your glory known to the ends of the earth."

> AS DISCIPLES WILLING TO FOLLOW JESUS, WE SURRENDER THE RIGHT TO DETERMINE THE DIRECTION OF OUR LIVES.

So the question is: Are we really willing to give God a blank check? To obey Him, no matter the cost? Let's examine ten reasons we should give God a blank check with our life:

1. JESUS IS WORTHY OF ABSOLUTE SURRENDER

As they were traveling on the road someone said to Him, "I will follow You wherever You go!"

Jesus told him, "Foxes have dens, and birds of the sky have nests, but the Son of Man has no place to lay His head." Then He said to another, "Follow Me."

"Lord," he said, "first let me go bury my father."

But He told him, "Let the dead bury their own dead, but you go and spread the news of the kingdom of God."

Another also said, "I will follow You, Lord, but first let me go and say good-bye to those at my house."

But Jesus said to him, "No one who puts his hand to the plow and looks back is fit for the kingdom of God" (Luke 9:57-62).

The same Jesus who said these words is the same Jesus we claim to follow! Are we willing to go anywhere, leave everything, and follow Him? Jesus is worthy of nothing less.

What does absolute surrender look like in your life? What must you give up?

2. JESUS IS WORKING TO ADVANCE HIS KINGDOM

I wrote the first narrative, Theophilus, about all that Jesus began to do and teach (Acts 1:1).

Notice the word "began." This was just the tip of the iceberg, the very beginning of all that Jesus would do. But there's a problem. Once we get to verse 11, Jesus is gone! But He doesn't stop advancing His kingdom.

How does Jesus continue to advance His kingdom throughout the Book of Acts?
1:24 *As the disciples pray, Jesus selects an apostle to replace Judas.*
2:33 _____.
2:47 _____.
9:5-10 _____.
9:34 _____.
13:2 _____.
13:11 _____.
16:14 _____.

How are you a part of what Jesus is doing in this world to advance His kingdom?

3. JESUS HAS CLOTHED EVERY CHRISTIAN WITH HIS POWER

"...stay in the city until you have been clothed with power from on high" (Luke 24:49, NIV).

Jesus told His disciples to wait in Jerusalem until He sent His Holy Spirit to divinely empower them for His mission. Jesus has clothed every single one of us with His power.

How is the power of Jesus evident in your life?

4. JESUS HAS GIVEN EVERY CHRISTIAN THE SAME PURPOSE

But you will receive power when the Holy Spirit has come on you, and you will be My witnesses..." (Acts 1:8a).

God clothes every single Christian with the power of His Spirit so that we might lead people to Christ. As followers of Christ filled with His Spirit, our responsibility is to proclaim the Word of God.

How does your life reflect this purpose? Is there anything you need to do, or decision you need to make, in order to be a witness of Jesus?

5. THE WORLD IS OUR GOAL

"...you will be My witnesses in Jerusalem, in all Judea and Samaria, and to the ends of the earth" (Acts 1:8b).

The Book of Acts closes in chapter 28 with the gospel going forward into new places where it had never been heard. And that is our goal today. You and I are the continuation of this story, and 2000 years later there are still millions of people who have not heard the gospel of Jesus.

What needs to change in your life in light of this goal?

6. THE WORD IS OUR GUARANTEE

During these days Peter stood up among the brothers—the number of people who were together was about 120—and said: "Brothers, the Scripture had to be fulfilled that the Holy Spirit through the mouth of David spoke in advance about Judas, who became a guide to those who arrested Jesus (Acts 1:15-16).

God fulfilled this promise He gave hundreds of years before. And God has promised you and me that He will empower us with His Spirit to be His witnesses "to the ends of the earth." Guaranteed.

How does knowing that God has promised in His Word to empower you and enable you impact how you think about His mission?

7. THE STAKES ARE HIGH

"Repent," Peter said to them, "and be baptized, each of you, in the name of Jesus Christ for the forgiveness of your sins, and you will receive the gift of the Holy Spirit. For the promise is for you and for your children, and for all who are far off, as many as the Lord our God will call." And with many other words he testified and strongly urged them, saying, "Be saved from this corrupt generation!" (Acts 2:38-40).

We are surrounded daily by people who are under the judgment of God. In His mercy, God sent His Son to pay the price for our sin so that everyone who turns from his sin and trusts in Jesus will be reconciled to God forever. This is the difference between everlasting life and eternal death.

What's more important to you? Your personal comfort or how those around you will spend their eternity? How does your life reflect this?

8. THE SPIRIT IS HERE

Suddenly a sound like that of a violent rushing wind came from heaven, and it filled the whole house where they were staying. And tongues, like flames of fire that were divided, appeared to them and rested on each one of them. Then they were all filled with the Holy Spirit... (Acts 2:2-4).

Every single follower of Christ is indwelled by the Spirit of Christ. The same Spirit who was active at Pentecost is the same Spirit who is living in you.

How does knowing the Holy Spirit is present in your life impact the way you live daily?

9. THE GLORY OF CHRIST LEAVES US NO OTHER OPTION

Yes, Yahweh, we wait for You in the path of Your judgments. Our desire is for Your name and renown (Isa. 26:8).

More than we want our comfort and traditions, even more than we want our own lives, we want His gospel and His glory known. And we are willing to give whatever He asks because we love Him.

What do you want more—your own comfort or for the gospel and glory of God to be known? What's the evidence of this in your life?

10. THE COMING OF CHRIST LEAVES US WITH GREAT ANTICIPATION

They said, "Men of Galilee, why do you stand looking up into heaven? This Jesus, who has been taken from you into heaven, will come in the same way that you have seen Him going into heaven" (Acts 1:11).

One day, our Savior, Lord, and King—the One whom we follow—is coming back for us. Let's be ready. Let's not be found holding onto the pleasures and pursuits of this world.

Do you live as if Christ could return any day? How does this shape the way you follow Him?

THE COST MIGHT BE GREAT, BUT THE REWARD IS FAR GREATER.

on what you studied.

Read 1 John 3:1.

For a time, my adopted son Caleb and I were doing this thing where I would point at him across the room and yell, "I love Caleb!" Then he would look back at me and yell, "I love Daddy!" One day we were doing this and Caleb was laughing until all of the sudden he stopped, looked at me, and asked, "You love me?"

I said, "Yeah, buddy, I do."
And then he asked what seems to be his favorite question: "Why?"
I said, "Because you're my son."
So he asked the question again: "Why?"

This time I thought to myself, Now that's a good question. Out of all the children in the world, why is this precious little boy standing in front of me my son? I thought about all the factors that had come together to lead my wife, Heather, and me to Kazakhstan where Caleb was an orphan. I thought about all the ups and downs where we wondered if we were ever going to have kids. I started tearing up and I could tell Caleb was confused, wondering if he should ever ask his daddy "why" again. But I looked back at him and said, "You're our son because we wanted you. And we came to get you so that you might have a mommy and a daddy."

Doesn't it take your breath away for a moment to hear God say, "I love you"? To which we, in our sinfulness, must certainly respond, "Why?" And then to hear Him answer, "Because you're My child." To which we ask the obvious question, "Why would I, a hopeless sinner, now be called Your cherished child?" Only to hear Him say, "Because I wanted you, and I came to get you so that you might know Me as Father."

How do you respond to God's love of you as His child?

Knowing that God loves you like this, is there any reason you wouldn't write Him a "blank check" with your life?

List three reasons why it would be hard to write God a blank check with your life right now.

What will it take to eliminate these barriers to giving your life fully to God?

Pray that you fully grasp God's mercy and love for you as His child.

Read Matthew 4:19.

A member of our church named Matthew served for many years alongside Christians in one of the most severely persecuted areas of the world. Coming to Christ in this almost exclusively Muslim nation was extremely costly. Matthew told me that on the first day men or women came to faith in Christ in that country, they were encouraged to make a list of all the unbelievers they knew (which was often practically everyone they knew).

Then they were encouraged to circle the names of the ten people on that list who were least likely to kill them for becoming a Christ-follower. Out of those ten remaining names, the new believers were encouraged to share the gospel with each one of them as soon as possible. That's exactly what they would do, and this is how the gospel was spreading in that country.

It sounds a lot like Matthew 4:19, doesn't it? "Follow Me," ... "and I will make you fish for people!" As soon as people become followers of Jesus, they begin fishing for men.

But sadly, this is not the case for many—maybe most—professing Christians in the world. Many have hardly ever shared the gospel of Jesus Christ with even one other person at any point in their Christian life. Even for those who have shared the gospel at some point, most are not actively leading people around them to follow Jesus.

Why is this the case? Why are so few followers of Christ personally fishing for men when this is designed to be central in every Christian's life? Could it be because we have fundamentally misunderstood the central purpose for which God created us? And could it be that as a result, we are completely missing one of the chief pleasures God has planned for us?

Have you ever shared the gospel? If not, why not?

If so, how did God shape you as a result of your obedience in sharing?

Pray that God would remind you of your purpose in Him and give you boldness to share the gospel with those around you.

GOD'S GLORY

As you follow Jesus, your primary goal is to give glory to God. There are many ways you probably already do this. To discover how you can give glory to God in every way, try the following this week:

Pick a single day of the week and journal your activities. For instance, if you eat lunch at noon write down where you ate and who you were with. Do this for as much of the day as you can.

Example daily journal entries:
7:30 am—woke up late, got dressed, headed for the bus
8:15 am—first class of the day, took a test
11:30 am—ate lunch in the cafeteria with friends
3:30 pm—got home from school and did the dishes
6:30 pm—hung out with friends and played Xbox
8:00 pm—did homework
11:00 pm—went to bed early

Look over your day and assess how you can give glory to God in all the activities of your life. For example, how can something as simple as eating lunch with friends bring glory to God? Was there an opportunity to serve someone, pray for someone, or help someone in any way during that time?

Think about how you could be more intentional throughout the week in glorifying God with your life. Use the space below to list some ways you can get started.

SESSION 5
THE CHURCH

THE CHURCH

It's impossible to follow Christ apart from joining his church. In fact, anyone who claims to be a Christian yet is not an active member of a church may not actually be a follower of Christ at all.

To some, maybe many, this may sound heretical. "Are you saying that joining a church makes someone a Christian?" you might ask. And I would answer, "Absolutely not." Joining a church most certainly does not make one a Christian.

At the same time, to identify your life with the person of Christ is to join your life with the people of Christ. To surrender your life to His commands is to commit your life to His church. It is biblically, spiritually, and practically impossible to be a disciple of Christ (and much less make disciples of Christ) apart from total devotion to a family of Christians.

What if I said to you, "Man, I love you, but have I ever told you how much I can't stand your wife?" Would you take that as a compliment? Similarly, isn't the church the body of Christ? What if my wife said to me, "David, I love you, but I can't stand your body." I can assure you that I wouldn't take that as a compliment.

It's impossible to follow Jesus fully without loving His bride selflessly, and it's impossible to think that we can enjoy Christ apart from His body. Jesus goes so far as to identify the church with himself when He asks Saul on the road to Damascus, "Saul, Saul, why are you persecuting Me?" (Acts 9:4). Saul hadn't persecuted Christ himself, but He had persecuted Christians, so in essence Jesus was saying, "When you mess with them, you mess with Me."

To come to Christ is to become a part of His church. Followers of Jesus have the privilege of being identified with His family. As we die to ourselves, we begin to live for others, and everything Christ does in us begins to affect everyone Christ puts around us. Recognizing this reality, and experiencing the relationships that God has designed for His people, specifically in the church, is essential to being a disciple and making disciples of all nations.

> HOW CAN WE DISPLAY THE GLORY OF THE ONE WHO SACRIFICED HIS LIFE FOR THE CHURCH IF WE SACRIFICE NOTHING FOR THE CHURCH?

Complete the viewer guide below as you watch DVD session 5.

The church is...

"a local body of baptized believers..."

Baptism is a declaration that we belong to _____.

In baptism, we also declare that we belong to _____ _____.

"joined together under biblical leadership..."

The church is _____ with servants of the Word.

The church is _____ to be servants with the Word.

"to grow in the likeness of Christ..."

Together in the church, we want to know the _____ of Christ.

Together in the church, we want to imitate the _____ of Christ.

Together in the church, we want to display the _____ of Christ.

"and express the love of Christ to each other and to the world around them."

_____ is the distinguishing mark of the church.

We commit our lives as members of local churches for the good of _____.

We commit our lives as members of local churches for the good of _____ _____.

We commit our lives as members of local churches for the good of _____.

We commit our lives as members of local churches for the _____ of _____.

RESPOND

The room was packed full of people, and the preacher held the audience in the palm of his hand. "I would like everyone to bow your heads and close your eyes," he said, and we all followed suit. He then declared: "Tonight, I want to call you to put your faith in God. Tonight, I am urging you to begin a personal relationship with Jesus for the first time in your life. Let me be clear," he said, "I'm not inviting you to join the church. I'm just inviting you to come to Christ." As the preacher passionately pleaded for personal decisions, scores of people stood from their seats and walked down the aisles of the auditorium to make a commitment to Christ.

Yet there was a serious problem in all of this. These people had been deceived. They had been told that it is possible to make a commitment to Christ apart from a commitment to the church.

> ### THE BIBLICAL REALITY IS THAT IT'S IMPOSSIBLE TO FOLLOW CHRIST APART FROM JOINING HIS CHURCH.

Therefore I, the prisoner for the Lord, urge you to walk worthy of the calling you have received, with all humility and gentleness, with patience, accepting one another in love, diligently keeping the unity of the Spirit with the peace that binds us. There is one body and one Spirit—just as you were called to one hope at your calling—one Lord, one faith, one baptism, one God and Father of all, who is above all and through all and in all.

Now grace was given to each one of us according to the measure of the Messiah's gift. For it says:

When He ascended on high,
He took prisoners into captivity;
He gave gifts to people.

But what does "He ascended" mean except that He descended to the lower parts of the earth? The One who descended is also the One who ascended far above all the heavens, that He might fill all things. And He personally gave some to be apostles, some prophets, some evangelists, some pastors and teachers, for the training of the saints in the work of ministry, to build up the body of Christ, until we all reach unity in the faith and in the knowledge of God's Son, growing into a mature man with a stature measured by Christ's fullness. Then we will no longer be little children, tossed by the waves and blown around by every wind of teaching, by human cunning with cleverness in the techniques of deceit. But speaking the truth in love, let us grow in every way into Him who is the head—Christ. From Him the whole body, fitted and knit together by every supporting ligament, promotes the growth of the body for building up itself in love by the proper working of each individual part (Eph. 4:1-16).

MINIMIZING THE CHURCH

There are many reasons we minimize the church today. As we look over some of these, ask yourself if you are guilty of minimizing the church in your life. Finish the sentences that follow each reason.

We are independent.
We tend to rely on ourselves rather than go to others for help and encouragement.

I am too independent when it comes to ...

When I understand the church's role in sharing life with others, it makes me ...

We are indifferent.
Is the local church really that big of a deal? We think we can just worship on our own.

I minimize gathering together with other believers by ...

When I understand the need to be with other Christians as a local church, I ...

We are immature.
Sometimes we minimize the church because we are simply immature in our faith.

I am acting spiritually immature when I ...

As a spiritually mature Christian, I will view the church as ...

We are indecisive.
We tend to move from church to church looking for the best "fit" when in reality we are looking for the better "deal." Church shopping is a product of our consumer mentality and creates an unhealthy view of the church.

I feel like the church should cater to my wants and needs, such as ...

When I view the church as the bride of Christ rather than a product or service, I ...

THE IMPORTANCE OF THE CHURCH

God's Word is clear when it comes to the role of the local church. Not only is the church extremely important, membership is vital. Let's look at the basic definition of what the local church is according to the book of Acts: **A local body of baptized believers joined together under biblical leadership to grow in the likeness of Christ and express the love of Christ to each other and to the world around them.**

How does this definition of the local church compare to your church?

What areas mentioned in this definition does your church excel in or struggle with?

While no church is perfect, it should be our desire to grow closer to Jesus and see Him shape and change our church just as He shapes us. Let's break down each component of this definition and really get a solid grasp of what it means to be a local church.

A local body of baptized believers...

> *There is one body and one Spirit—just as you were called to one hope at your calling* **(Eph. 4:4).**

The church at Ephesus was made up of Jewish and Gentile Christians who were experiencing division and tension, and Paul went to great lengths to make it clear to them that to be united to Christ is to be united to each other in the church.

joined together under biblical leadership...

> *And He personally gave some to be apostles, some prophets, some evangelists, some pastors and teachers, for the training of the saints in the work of ministry, to build up the body of Christ* **(Eph. 4:11-12).**

The primary role of leaders in the church is to serve God's people with God's Word. Church leaders are not intended to be the only ones doing ministry; they equip people in the church to minister.

to grow in the likeness of Christ...

> *until we all reach unity in the faith and in the knowledge of God's Son, growing into a mature man with a stature measured by Christ's fullness* (Eph. 4:13).

We gather together because we want to know Christ, and we need each other to know the truth. We also need each other to keep us from wandering from the truth, so that we can grow in maturity into Him who is the head, Christ. In doing this, the church displays God's glory to the world.

and express the love of Christ to each other and to the world around them.

> *with all humility and gentleness, with patience, accepting one another in love* (Eph. 4:2).

> *But speaking the truth in love, let us grow in every way into Him who is the head—Christ. From Him the whole body, fitted and knit together by every supporting ligament, promotes the growth of the body for building up itself in love by the proper working of each individual part* (Eph. 4:15-16).

> *"By this all people will know that you are My disciples, if you have love for one another"* (John 13:35).

Why join a church? Because of love. Love for who? Love for ourselves, other Christians, and non-Christians—for the glory of God.

YOU AND THE CHURCH

What local church are you, as a Christian, committed to? I encourage you to do whatever is necessary to commit your life as a member of a local body of baptized believers.

As a follower of Jesus, how are you giving your life in love for your church?

LOVE IS THE DISTINGUISHING MARK OF THE CHURCH.

REFLECT

on what you studied.

Read 1 Corinthians 12:15-26.

There's a trend that's developed today known as "dating the church." There's even a great book by Joshua Harris titled *Stop Dating the Church.* This phrase is a reference to how in our consumer-driven church market, we've developed the practice of hopping from one church to the next, attending this church or that church based on how we feel on that particular Sunday morning, or maybe just substituting other spiritual activities for the church in our lives. After all, we're Christians. We're a part of the church around the world. Why would we need to commit to one local church, anyway?

We date the church for a variety of reasons. We're independent, self-reliant, self-sufficient people, and the thought of mutual submission, accountability, and interdependence seems somewhat foreign, if not outright frightening. In addition, we're indecisive. We date different churches because we can't decide on one we really like. It's our consumer mentality applied to church shopping: looking for the best product with the best price on Sunday morning. We're always looking for the better deal, which often leads to a fairly critical attitude toward the church. We can find something wrong with every church we visit, and even when we do settle down somewhere, we're ever cognizant of the things we don't like.

On a whole, we're often indifferent. Is joining and committing to a local church really that big a deal? Isn't it just a formality, and an unnecessary formality, at that? Many professing Christians simply have no idea why dating the church would be wrong and why devotion to the church would be necessary.

Are you currently "dating the church"—attending more than one because you like different things about each? How has this affected the way you view the local church as a whole?

Do you agree with David Platt that "dating the church" is a result of not understanding the church in the first place? Why or why not?

As a result of this study, what will you do differently to support the local church where you are currently a member?

Pray about the church you attend, that you and your attitude toward Christ's bride would glorify God.

Read Ephesians 1:18-23.

According to Scripture, when people in the world see the life of Christ in the church, they will believe the love of God for the world. This is yet one more reason why every follower of Christ must be committed to the church: so that the glory of God might be made known in the world. This is the ultimate reason why every follower of Christ is a member of a church: because every disciple of Jesus desires to display the glory of God.

You may be tempted to think, *Well, can't I live for God's glory on my own?* And there's certainly a sense in which we are intended to display the glory of God in everything we do. But the message of God's Word is that God's glory is most majestically displayed not through you or through me, but through us. God raises up the church and says to all creation in the heavens, on the earth, and under the earth, "This is the bride and body of my Son, bought and purchased by His blood, to be my people and receive my power and enjoy my presence and declare my praise forever and ever."

It is a privilege to be a part of the church. To come to Christ is to become a member of His community. It is biblically, spiritually, and practically impossible to be a disciple of Christ (and much less make disciples of Christ) apart from total devotion to a family of Christians. For as Christians lock their arms and lives together with one another in local churches, nothing has the power to stop the global spread of God's gospel to the ends of the earth.

Do you think someone can be a disciple of Jesus' and not be a part of the church? Why or why not?

How does the church reach the world more effectively than people acting individually?

What is the significance of the church in your life?

Pray that God will be glorified by your local church as you display the love of Christ to the world.

CHURCH UP

As a member of a local church, you have a responsibility. Your connection to the local church is key to your walk with Jesus and your relationships with those around you. This week, let's assess your involvement and attitude toward the church. This assessment will help you get a better grasp of how you can share God's love as a member of the church.

As you go throughout your week, take time to consider the following questions:

1. **How involved in my church am I? Do I contribute to the ministry of the church, or am I only a consumer?**

2. **In what areas could I serve my church better? How can I get more information about the needs of the church?**

3. **How can I use my unique gifts and abilities to serve my church?**

4. **Is there any negative attitude or thought I have that I need to ask God to help me change so that I can better serve my church?**

5. **How connected am I to other people in my church? How can I connect better with others in my local church?**

6. **How can I set a positive example for others in my local church?**

7. **Does my involvement in the ministry of my church help display God's love to the world? If not, what do I need to change?**

Pray that you will have a passion to share God's love as a member of the church.

SESSION 6
OUR MISSION

OUR MISSION

Remember those four fishermen in Matthew 4? Peter, Andrew, James, and John. They chose to follow Jesus. And the Bible says they turned the world upside down. I want to be a part of a movement like that. I don't want to spend my life focused on church activities and buildings and designing programs for comfortable churchgoers. Nor do I want to build a kingdom that revolves around my limited gifts and imperfect leadership. I want to be a part of a people who really believe that we have the Spirit of God in each of us for the spread of the gospel through all of us. I want to be a part of a people who are gladly sacrificing the pleasures, pursuits, and possessions of this world because we are living for treasure in the world to come. I want to be a part of a people who have forsaken every earthly ambition in favor of one eternal aspiration: to see disciples made and churches multiplied from our houses to our communities to our cities to the nations.

This kind of movement involves all of us. Every single follower of Christ fishing for men. Every single disciple making disciples. No more spectators. Instead, ordinary people spreading the gospel in extraordinary ways all over the world. People from diverse backgrounds with different gifts and distinct platforms making disciples and multiplying churches through every domain of society in every place on the planet. This is God's design for His church, and disciples of Jesus must not settle for anything less.

THIS IS NOT A COMFORTABLE CALL FOR MOST CHRISTIANS TO COME, BE BAPTIZED, AND SIT IN ONE LOCATION. THIS IS A COSTLY COMMAND FOR EVERY CHRISTIAN TO GO, BAPTIZE, AND MAKE DISCIPLES OF ALL NATIONS.

Complete the viewer guide below as you watch DVD session 6.

As disciples of Jesus, let's believe in the authority of Christ.

Jesus is not just the _____ Lord and Savior over us.

Jesus is the _____ Lord and Savior over all.

He has authority over all nature and all _____.

He has authority over disease and _____.

He has authority over sin and _____.

He has authority over _____ _____.

He has authority over _____ life.

Jesus' authority compels us to go.

His worth is the _____ of our mission.

His worship is the _____ of our mission.

Jesus' authority gives us confidence as we go.

The gospel will _____.

The mission will _____.

Jesus' introduction in Matthew 4 shows that every follower of Jesus is a fisher of men. Jesus' conclusion in Matthew 28 shows that every disciple is a disciple-maker. Simply, to be a disciple is to make disciples. Some of the most common and yet most ignored words in all of Scripture may be Matthew 28:16-20. Jesus gathered His disciples on a mountain and gave them some final instructions. Called the Great Commission, these words should be at the center of everything we do as followers of Christ and as the church.

> *The 11 disciples traveled to Galilee, to the mountain where Jesus had directed them. When they saw Him, they worshiped, but some doubted. Then Jesus came near and said to them, "All authority has been given to Me in heaven and on earth. Go, therefore, and make disciples of all nations, baptizing them in the name of the Father and of the Son and of the Holy Spirit, teaching them to observe everything I have commanded you. And remember, I am with you always, to the end of the age"* **(Matt. 28:16-20).**

Notice how Jesus starts with a claim: "All authority has been given to Me..."

What authority is Jesus talking about?

Who does He have authority over? Explain.

How does Jesus' authority impact you and me as we follow Him on a daily basis?

JESUS IS NOT JUST THE PERSONAL SAVIOR AND LORD OVER US; HE'S THE UNIVERSAL LORD AND SAVIOR OVER ALL. SO WE'RE COMPELLED TO GO, AND WE'RE CONFIDENT AS WE GO.

AS A DISCIPLE OF JESUS...

Based on the authority of Jesus, we are to follow this Great Commission. A commission is an assignment or mission. There is no room for doubt as to what Jesus has called us to do. Let's break down the different elements of the Great Commission so we can better understand them and how they apply to following Jesus.

"Go..."

Our mission begins with action. Following Jesus requires action. Just as the first disciples left their families and jobs and walked with Jesus, we are to walk with Him wherever He leads as well. It is not comfortable, nor is it easy, but it is the first step of God's mission for every Christian on earth.

How does the word "Go" apply to your daily life as a disciple of Jesus?

Define what "Go" looks like for you:
Example: As I go to my classes at school...

"...make disciples of all nations"

Notice that there is a firm statement by Jesus about making disciples. This is not a question. We don't have to wonder what He is saying. Clearly, disciples of Jesus are to make more disciples of Jesus.

Have you ever made a disciple of Jesus? What were the circumstances and how did the conversation go?

How can we help make disciples of all nations from where we are?

"…baptizing them in the name of the Father and of the Son and of the Holy Spirit"
Baptism is the identifiable beginning of a new disciple's journey to follow Jesus.

Have you been baptized? If not, why not?

If you have been baptized, what did it mean to you?

How would you explain baptism to someone who wanted to know what it is and why they should do it?

"…teaching them to observe everything I have commanded you."
Many skip over this crucial part of the Great Commission. Jesus doesn't just tell us to teach disciples, but to teach them to observe all that He has commanded. This means that the discipleship process will take time. Rather than seeing someone baptized and sent on their way with a Bible or a brochure, Jesus tells us here to actively involve ourselves in walking new followers of Jesus through His teachings.

What could be the result of skipping over this important part of the Great Commission?

How can you teach someone to observe everything Christ has commanded?

CAN I REALLY DO THIS?

Perhaps you have always thought that there are those who are gifted to make disciples and those who aren't. The truth is that every follower of Jesus is not just called but commanded to make disciples. If you are nervous or apprehensive about it, it could be because you have placed the pressure of "success" or "failure" on your abilities to persuade others to believe. The good news is that you are not called to convert people, but simply to share God's love with them.

Making disciples is based on who Jesus is and what He can do. It's not based on who you are and what you can do. Jesus requires our obedience, but He will do the work!

What is the greatest obstacle in your way of making disciples?

How can having a right view of who God is help you overcome this obstacle?

FOLLOW ME

Over the last six weeks we have looked at what is means to be a disciple of Jesus, from leaving everything behind to dying to ourselves, taking up our cross, and walking after Him. As Christians, we are to take part in the greatest mission of all time, the Great Commission. Every disciple of Jesus has been called, loved, created, and saved to make disciples of Jesus who make disciples of Jesus who make disciples of Jesus until the grace of God is enjoyed and the glory of God is exalted among every people group on the planet. And on that day, every disciple of Jesus—every true and authentic follower of Christ and fisher of men—will see the Savior's face and behold the Father's splendor in a scene of indescribable beauty and everlasting bliss that will never, ever fade away.

THIS IS A CALL WORTH DYING FOR.
THIS IS A KING WORTH LIVING FOR.
WILL YOU FOLLOW HIM?

Read Matthew 28:19-20.

Imagine your church. Don't picture the building or parking lot, and don't envision the activities and programs. Just the people. Whether there are 50, 100, 500, or 5,000, simply imagine the people who comprise your church.

Now imagine a people living in a world of sin and rebellion, suffering and pain. A world where over three billion men, women, and children survive on less than two dollars a day, and a billion of those people live in absolute poverty—in remote villages and city slums where hundreds of millions are starving and dying of preventable diseases. A world where billions of people are engrossed in false religions, and around two billion of them have never even heard the gospel. They are all (literally billions of people) on a road that leads to an eternal hell—suffering for sin that will never, ever, ever end.

But you and the people in your church have been transformed by the gospel of Christ. In your minds, you know that Jesus died on the cross and rose from the grave to save people from their sins. In your hearts, you have tasted and seen that He alone can satisfy people's souls. Your wills are now abandoned to His ways, and you long to be His witnesses throughout the world. God has banded you together as brothers and sisters in a local church with a global commission: make disciples of all nations. God has filled every single one of you with the power of His own Spirit to enable each of you individually and all of you collectively to reach the world with the gospel.

So, if you had nothing but people—no buildings, no programs, no staff, and no activities—and you were charged with spreading the gospel to the whole world, where would you begin? Would you build buildings? Would you hire amazing speakers and a talented staff? Would you institute programs? You would probably not do any of these things. And neither would I. Instead, we would all go. Every single one of us. We would scatter as rapidly as possible to make the gospel known to as many people as possible.

How does it make you feel to know that the eternity of billions of people is at stake?

In what ways do these urgent stakes impact you as a follower of Jesus?

How can your life show the world that you understand these urgent stakes?

Pray that God will open the eyes of every Christian to the urgency of taking the gospel to the world.

Read Matthew 4:18-22.

I have a brother in Christ named Rajesh. Rajesh lives in Bihar, India, the home to the poorest of the poor in India; this state's death rate is approximately 5,000 people per day. Rajesh estimates that approximately 0.1% of people in Bihar are evangelical Christians. Based on the truth of God's Word, that means approximately 4,995 people in Rajesh's state plunge into everlasting torment every single day.

Rajesh and his wife's deepest passion is declaring the gospel to people around them. But three years ago, Rajesh was struggling in his faith. Facing resistance to the gospel on all sides, he wondered if anyone around him would ever come to faith in Christ.

One day, though, Rajesh was freshly challenged to make disciples. He was encouraged to find a completely unreached village (i.e., no church or Christians among them), walk into that village, and say to anyone he met, "I am here in the name of Jesus, and I would like to pray for you and your home." Rajesh thought it was a crazy idea and that it would never work, but he was at the end of his rope, so he decided to try it.

At the first village Rajesh entered, a man approached him, and Rajesh began his pre-scripted introduction: "I am here in the name of Jesus…" Before Rajesh could finish the rest of what he was saying, the man interrupted him and said, "Jesus? I have heard a little about him. Can you tell me more?" Rajesh was shocked. "I can," he said. The man replied, "Well, wait a moment. I'd like to get my family and some friends to hear what you have to say."

Dumbfounded, Rajesh walked with the man to his home, and within a matter of minutes, a variety of villagers had gathered together there. Rajesh shared the gospel, and the people said they wanted to hear more. Within a few weeks, 25 of them had trusted in Christ as King. But the story does not end there. Rajesh encouraged those 25 people to find villages where they could do the same thing he had done. As a result, since that day approximately 150 churches have been planted in 150 different villages.

Does Rajesh's story encourage you in sharing the gospel? How?

What could you do in your home, school, or city to reach people as boldly as Rajesh did?

What might happen if you were really determined to follow Jesus as a radical disciple?

Pray for a heart that passionately desires to follow Jesus, no matter the cost, for the sake of the gospel.

MAKING DISCIPLES

Jesus left an example for us as to how to make disciples. He took a dozen men and invested in their lives. Within that group, He took three and really invested heavily. The method was and is very simple, pour into a few others who will in turn pour into a few more. This plan is not just a great idea; it's the God of the universe's strategy to reach the world with the gospel!

In the circles below, include the names of a few people you might begin to pour into. You may not be their official "leader" but you can be a positive influence in their lives for the gospel. The goal is to develop others into disciple-makers capable of going out and reaching others.

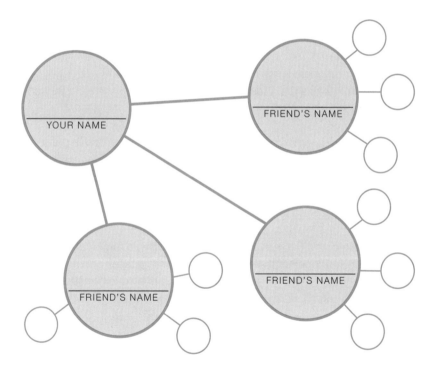

Begin by praying that these three individuals will be receptive to your influence in their lives.

Be up front and ask them if they would like to follow Jesus together as a group of disciple-makers.

Think of intentional ways you can live out the gospel with these individuals.

PERSONAL DISCIPLE-MAKING PLAN

THE DISCIPLE'S PLAN

Wherever you find a Christian who is not leading men and women to Christ, something is very wrong. To be a disciple of Jesus is to make disciples of Jesus. This has been true ever since the first century when Jesus invited four men to follow Him. His words have echoed throughout history: "Follow Me, and I will make you fishers of men."

More important than searching for fish all over the sea, these men would spread the gospel all over the world. They would give their lives not simply to being disciples of Jesus, but sacrificially to making disciples of Jesus. And God's design for twenty-first century disciples is exactly the same. He calls every disciple of Jesus to make disciples of Jesus who make disciples of Jesus until the gospel penetrates every people group in the world.

But something is wrong. Very wrong. Somewhere along the way, we have lost sight of what it means to be a disciple and we have laid aside Jesus' command to make disciples. We have tragically minimized what it means to be His follower, and we have virtually ignored the biblical expectation that we fish for men. The result is a rampant spectator mentality that skews discipleship across the church, stifles the spread of the gospel around the world, and ultimately sears the heart of what it means for each of us to be a Christian.

I don't share all of this to make you feel guilty. My hope is that you have a desire to see people come to know Christ through your life. If so, will you take some intentional steps toward that goal?

DEVELOP YOUR PLAN

To follow Jesus is to believe Jesus, and in order to believe Jesus, we must listen to Jesus. The life of the disciple is the life of a learner. We constantly attune our ears to the words of our Master. As He teaches us through His Word, He transforms us in the world. As you develop your personal plan, examine six areas of disciple-making:

1. HOW WILL I FILL MY MIND WITH TRUTH?

To follow Jesus our lives must be filled with the truth of God. Begin your plan by answering the following questions.

In what ways can I adjust my daily schedule around reading God's Word?
You might start with a plan to read a chapter a day. Consider using an intentional Bible reading plan that covers all of Scripture over a certain period of time.

How can I begin to effectively memorize Scripture?
As you read, look for verses, paragraphs, or even chapters that seem particularly significant and applicable to your life. Then commit them to memory.

What steps will I take to learn the truth in God's Word from others?
Reading, studying, and understanding the Bible is not just an individual effort; it's a community project. We all need pastors who are teaching God's Word faithfully to us. And we all need brothers and sisters who are consistently encouraging us with God's Word.

2. HOW WILL I FUEL MY AFFECTIONS FOR GOD?

There is a dangerous tendency for discipline in the disciple's life to become mechanical and monotonous. Our aim is not simply to know God; our aim is to love God. The more we read His Word, the more we delight in His glory.

How will I worship God?

To the church at Corinth, Paul says, "Whether you eat or drink, or whatever you do, do all to the glory of God" (1 Cor. 10:31). So consider general ways that you might focus on worship in every facet of your life. Then meet regularly with the church for worship.

How will I pray?

Jesus said, "When you pray, go into your room and shut the door and pray to your Father who is in secret" (Matthew 6:6). In other words, find yourself a place and set aside a time to be with the Father.

How will I give?

According to Jesus, our money doesn't just reflect our hearts; our hearts actually follow our money. One of the most effective ways to fuel affection for God is to give your resources in obedience to God.

3. HOW WILL I SHARE GOD'S LOVE AS A WITNESS IN THE WORLD?

God's will in the world and for our lives is to spread His gospel, grace, and glory to all peoples. Instead of asking what God's will is for our lives, every disciple of Jesus asks, "How can my life align with His will for me to be His witness in the world?" This general question leads us to more specific questions.

Who will you share with?

You are surrounded by people who are not Christians. So take a minute to write down the names of three, five, or maybe ten unbelievers God has placed in your life. Then begin praying specifically for God through the power of his Spirit to draw them to His salvation.

How will you share?

In the context of where you live, work, and play, and with the people God has put around you (including the names of those you listed above), how can you begin to speak intentionally about God's character, man's sin, Christ's provision, and our need to respond to that provision?

When will you share?

Instead of passively sitting back and waiting for people to mysteriously ask you about Jesus, it's wise to consider how you can actively show Christ's love by creating opportunities to tell people about Jesus. How can you specifically and deliberately create opportunities to share the gospel?

4. HOW WILL I SPREAD GOD'S GLORY AMONG ALL PEOPLES?

What will your part be in reaching the nations? Jesus has called us to think beyond our local friends and family and have a heart for the nations. Visit the International Mission Board website *(www.imb.org)* to learn about specific people groups who need your prayers and support.

How will I pray for the nations?

Let's pray passionately for God's kingdom to come and will to be done across the earth. Plan to deliberately focus your praying generally on the nations and specifically on the unreached people groups of the world.

How will I give to the nations?

How will you sacrifice the wants in your budget to give to the needs of the world—particularly the need for every people group to hear the gospel? Plan to spend for the sake of the nations.

How will I go to the nations?
Some unreached people groups have actually come to America and may be in your community, so consider ways you might reach out to them. Then consider ways you might cross the ocean to go to them, whether that's on a short-term trip for a week or a few months in the summer.

5. HOW WILL I SHOW GOD'S LOVE AS A MEMBER OF A CHURCH?

How will your connection as a member of the local church further the gospel? Lock arms with a local church, not as a spectator on the sidelines, but as a participant in the mission.

What church will I commit to as a member?
Is this the local body of Christ where you can most effectively make disciples of Christ?

What will I do within the church to serve as a part of the body?
As you look across the church of which you are a member, consider what things you can do to build up that body of Christ.

6. HOW WILL I MAKE DISCIPLE-MAKERS AMONG A FEW PEOPLE?

God may lead us to live in all kinds of different places in the world. Yet regardless of where we live, the task we have is the same: God has commanded every disciple to make disciples. Think about a few people you could disciple.

How will I gather the group?
Consider two, three, or four people that God has put in your sphere of influence. Then invite those few people to spend time with you in the days ahead for the express purpose of growing in Christ together.

How will I teach them to obey God's Word?
Maybe you read through a Bible book together, or maybe you use some other sort of tool for Bible study. Don't settle for simply teaching them information. Focus on seeing transformation.

How will I model obedience to God's Word?
As you focus your life on the few people God has given you, they need to see and hear and sense the life of Christ in you. So invite them into your home. Let them see you with your family. Show them how to pray, study the Bible, and share the gospel.

How will I send them out to make disciples themselves? *The goal is not just for these few people that you are focused on to follow Jesus; the goal is for them to fish for men. You continue to encourage, serve, teach, care for, and pray for them, but you also release them to take time they have spent with you and begin to spend it with others doing the same thing you have done.*

NO CHILD OF GOD IS INTENDED BY GOD TO BE SIDELINED AS A SPECTATOR IN THE GREAT COMMISSION. EVERY CHILD OF GOD HAS BEEN INVITED BY GOD TO BE ON THE FRONT LINES OF THE SUPREME MISSION IN ALL OF HISTORY.

WRITE YOUR PLAN

Over the course of this study, you have been asked to complete six activities in the "ENGAGE" section of each session. Each activity is one part of this personal disciple-making strategy. Go back through your study guide and look at each week and see how you have assessed each area of the strategy. Then review your responses in the previous activity and use the space below to summarize your plan to follow Jesus and make disciples.

1. How I will fill my mind with truth:

_____

_____

2. How I will fuel my affections for God:

_____

_____

3. How I will share God's love as a witness in the world:

_____

_____

4. How I will spread God's glory among all people:

_____

_____

5. How I will share God's love as a member of the church:

_____

_____

6. How I will make disciple-makers among a few people:

_____

_____

Put this plan somewhere you will see it daily, such as in your locker or on your bathroom mirror, and assess it throughout the year. Remember, the goal is to glorify God as you follow Jesus and make disciples.